The Children's Book of Angels

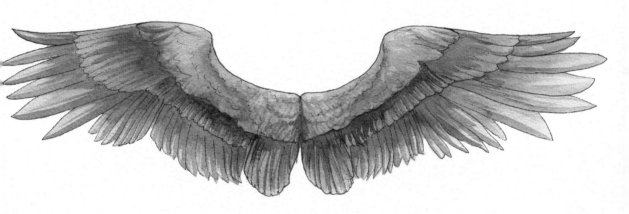

ILLUSTRATED BY
Austyn Schwartzbeck

WRITTEN BY
Jerry Windley-Daoust

Printed in the United States of America
First Edition: ISBN: 978-1-944008-67-3

Published by Holy Heroes, LLC.
www.HolyHeroes.com

Other books by Jerry Windley-Daoust:
77 Ways to Pray with Your Kids
The All Saints' Day Party
The Catholic Family Book of Prayers
The Illuminated Rosary
Lectio Divina for Teens

Angels are all around you. But they are usually invisible.

God made each angel for a particular purpose, to live a particular role—just like He made you for a special reason that only you can fulfill.

And did you know that God made one angel to watch over you and to help you every day?

Read on to learn many more wonderful things about God's holy angels!

When Did God Make the Angels?

Before God made the sun and the stars, the moon and the sea, and all the creatures of the world, He made the angels.

Who Are the Angels?

In some ways, angels are like people. They think their own thoughts and feel their own feelings. They travel on journeys and have adventures along the way.

Each angel has a name and a story. And like us, angels can be good or bad.

But in other ways, angels are not like us at all.

For one thing, they do not have bodies. They are spiritual creatures.

Because angels do not have bodies, they do not have to eat or sleep. They do not get married or have babies. And angels never die; they live forever.

What Do Angels Look Like?

Because angels do not have bodies, we cannot see them or touch them, except for sometimes when God reveals their presence to us.

Angels always see God. What must that be like?

God is beautiful, more beautiful than any art or song you can imagine, shining with love brighter than the sun. Being with God in this way makes the angels beautiful, too. Seeing God is so wonderful, the angels can't help but sing songs of praise!

Songs of the Angels

"Glory to God in the highest and on earth peace to those on whom His favor rests."
(Luke 2:13-14)

"Holy, holy, holy is the Lord of hosts! All the earth is filled with His glory!"
(Isaiah 6:3)

"Great and wonderful are Your works, Lord God almighty...."
(Revelation 15:3)

What Do Angels Do?

Angels are the servants and messengers of God. They share God's words with His people and help Him save the world from sin. Sin separates people from God, and it causes death. So helping God save the world from sin is very important work!

How Do Angels Announce God's Good News?

The Bible tells many stories about how God sent angels to announce good news.

Once, God visited a husband and wife named Abraham and Sarah. The Lord and two of His angels appeared to them disguised as travelers. Abraham and Sarah invited the strangers to stop, rest, and eat.

The Lord appeared to Abraham by the oak of Mamre, as he sat in the entrance of his tent, while the day was growing hot. Looking up, he saw three men standing near him.
(Genesis 18:1-2)

The visitors told Abraham and Sarah
that they would soon have a baby boy.

That news made Sarah laugh! She thought
that she was too old to have a baby.

But one of them said to Sarah,
"Why do you laugh? Is anything
too marvelous for the Lord to do?"

Mary said, "Behold, I am the handmaid of the Lord. May it be done to me according to your word."

Then the angel departed from her.
(Luke 1:38)

Many years later, God sent an archangel named Gabriel to a young woman of Nazareth named Mary. Gabriel told Mary that she, too, would give birth to a son by the power of the Holy Spirit. That baby was Jesus.

On the night when Jesus was born, an angel appeared to some shepherds to tell them the good news.

The angel of the Lord appeared to them and the glory of the Lord shone around them, and they were struck with great fear. The angel said to them, "Do not be afraid; for behold, I proclaim to you good news of great joy that will be for all the people. For today in the city of David a savior has been born for you who is Messiah and Lord ..."

(Luke 2:9-11)

How Do Angels Help People?

Sometimes God sends angels to help people.

Once, when a young man named Tobias was sent by his father on a dangerous journey to a far-away city, God sent the Archangel Raphael to go with him.

Raphael helped Tobias safely complete his journey. Then he helped Tobias marry a young woman named Sarah and defeat a demon named Asmodeus. He even helped Tobias catch a fish that cured his father's blindness!

At the end of this happy story, Raphael revealed who he really was—an angel sent by God.

"God sent me to heal you and your daughter-in-law Sarah. I am Raphael, one of the seven angels who stand and serve before the Glory of the Lord."
(Tobit 12:14-15)

How Do Angels Bring People Hope?

God also sends angels to strengthen people and give them hope.

He sent an angel to help a woman named Hagar and her son when they were lost in the desert. The angel showed her where to find water and let her know that God was watching over her.

God's angel called to Hagar from Heaven: "What is the matter, Hagar? Do not fear...." Then God opened her eyes, and she saw a well of water. She went and filled the skin with water, and then let the boy drink. *(Genesis 21:17, 19)*

And when the prophet Elijah was discouraged about his mission and wanted to give up, God sent an angel to strengthen him with special bread and water.

…the angel of the Lord…touched [Elijah], and said, "Get up and eat or the journey will be too much for you!" He got up, ate, and drank; then strengthened by that food, he walked forty days and forty nights to the mountain of God, Horeb.

(1 Kings 19:7-8)

How Do Angels Rescue People?

God sends angels to free his people, too.

When the Egyptian pharaoh made slaves of God's people, God sent an angel to fight the Egyptians so that his people could go free.

And when King Herod arrested Peter for telling people about Jesus, God sent an angel to free him in the middle of the night. The angel took off Peter's chains, opened the doors of the prison, and made him invisible to the guards!

Then Peter recovered his senses and said, "Now I know for certain that [the] Lord sent His angel and rescued me from the hand of Herod…."
(Acts 12:11)

What Are Demons?

Angels can choose to be good or bad. Angels who choose to reject God are called *demons*. Demons think they are better than God.

The most powerful of the demons is Satan, or the Devil.

The Bible tells about a great battle in Heaven between the good angels and the demons. The Archangel Michael was the leader of the good angels, and through the power God, they defeated Satan and the other demons and cast them out of Heaven.

> Michael and his angels battled against the dragon. The dragon and its angels fought back, but they did not prevail and there was no longer any place for them in Heaven.
>
> *(Revelation 12:7-8)*

Even though the forces of evil are powerful, God is always stronger. God sent His Son, Jesus, to defeat Satan and the demons once and for all. They thought they could defeat God by killing Jesus on a cross, but they were wrong! By His sacrifice, Jesus changed His Cross from a sign of death to a sign of love.

Any time you are afraid of evil, ask Jesus and His angels for help.

Prayer to St. Michael

St. Michael the Archangel, defend us in battle. Be our protection against the wickedness and snares of the devil. May God rebuke him, we humbly pray; and do Thou, O Prince of the Heavenly Host, by the power of God, cast into Hell Satan and all the evil spirits who prowl about the world seeking the ruin of souls. Amen.

Do Angels Always Look Like a Person with Two Wings?

Sometimes, the angels who appeared to the prophets looked very strange indeed. The prophet Ezekiel saw angels called Cherubim, each of which had four sets of wings and four faces: the face of a human, an ox, an eagle, and a lion.

The prophet Isaiah saw angels called Seraphim standing before the throne of God. These creatures had six wings: two covering their face, two covering their feet, and two for flying.

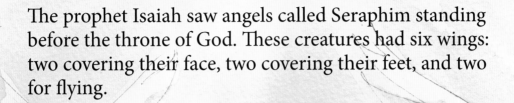

And the Apostle John was visited by an angel with a sword coming out of his mouth!

The hair of his head was as white as white wool or as snow, and his eyes were like a fiery flame. His feet were like polished brass refined in a furnace, and his voice was like the sound of rushing water. In his right hand he held seven stars. A sharp two-edged sword came out of his mouth, and his face shone like the sun at its brightest.

(Revelation 1:14-16).

Are All Angels Alike?

St. Thomas Aquinas studied angels so deeply, he is often called "the Angelic Doctor." He said that the angels all have their own "office"—a special job or role. He identified nine different orders (called "choirs") of angels.

2

Cherubim
These are the angels described by Ezekiel. The Israelites placed statues of Cherubim inside the Temple.

7

Principalities
These angels guide and protect nations and groups of people.

5

Virtues or Strongholds
These angels represent God's power in the world. They are in charge of the natural world and are associated with miracles.

8

Archangels
Three of the archangels appear in the Bible: Michael, Gabriel, and Raphael. The Church celebrates the feast of these three Archangels on September 29.

9

Angels
These angels protect people, carrying their prayers to God and accompanying their souls into God's presence when they die.

1

Seraphim
These are the angels seen by the prophet Isaiah. They stand before God, constantly praising Him.

3

Thrones or Elders
These strange-looking creatures are circles covered with eyes. They are living symbols of God's justice and authority.

6

Powers
These warrior angels protect the order of the physical universe and fight evil spirits.

4

Dominions
These angels are responsible for organizing the work of all the other angels below them.

> Now our knowledge of the angels is imperfect. ... But if we knew the offices and distinctions of the angels perfectly, we should know perfectly that each angel has his own office and his own order among things, and much more so than any star, though this be hidden from us.
>
> *Thomas Aquinas, Summa Theologica,*
> *Question 108, Article 3*

Who Are the Guardian Angels?

Jesus once told His disciples about the angels who watch over children (Matthew 18:10). We call these the Guardian Angels. Their job is to help us know and serve God and to protect us from spiritual danger.

Saint Josephine Bakhita once saw her guardian angel. When she was a young girl, she and a friend ran away from the man who had kidnapped them into slavery. But when Bakhita and her friend got lost in the woods at night, a beautiful angel appeared in the sky to comfort Bakhita and show her the right way to go.

The Angel of God Prayer

Angel of God, my guardian dear,
to whom God's love commits me here,
ever this day, be at my side,
to light and guard, to rule and guide.
Amen.

How Can You Find Angels?

If you want to go where lots of angels are, go to Mass.

During Mass, angels join us in praising Jesus Christ in the Holy Eucharist. Listen for when the priest invites us to join the angels in singing: "Glory to God in the highest, and on earth peace to people of good will…."

In her liturgy, the Church joins with the angels to adore the thrice-holy God.

Catechism of the Catholic Church, 335

You may never see an angel in this life, but you can pray that, through the help of the Holy Spirit and the angels, you might remain in God's friendship. And if you do, then one day you will know the beauty and glory of God, face to face . . . just like all of His angels.

To learn even more about angels visit:

HolyHeroes.com/Angels